130 Prayers for
Junior and Senior
High Schools

Let's Begin With Prayer

Mitch Finley

AVE MARIA PRESS Notre Dame, Indiana 46556

Dedication

For all the Catholic schools I attended: Saints Peter and Paul
School, Grangeville, Idaho; Saint Patrick's School and DeSales
High School, Walla Walla, Washington; Santa Clara
University, Santa Clara, California; and Marquette University,
Milwaukee, Wisconsin.

"For the LORD gives wisdom; from his mouth come
knowledge and understanding; he stores up sound wisdom
for the upright; he is a shield to those who walk blamelessly,
guarding the paths of justice and preserving the way of his
faithful ones" (Proverbs 2:6-8).

The Scripture quotations contained herein are from the *New Revised Standard Version Bible:
Catholic Edition*, copyright 1993 and 1989 by the National Council of the Churches of Christ
in the U.S.A. Used by permission. All rights reserved.

© 1997 by Ave Maria Press, Inc.

International Standard Book Number: 0-87793-615-3

Cover and text design by Elizabeth French

Printed and bound in the United States of America.

Library of Congress Cataloging-in-Publication Data

Finley, Mitch.
        Let's begin with prayer : 130 prayers for junior and senior high schools /
    Mitch Finley.
                    p.   cm.
        Includes index.
        ISBN 0-87793-615-3
        1. Schools—Prayers. 2. Catholic schools—Prayer-books and devotions—
English. 3. High school students—Prayer-books and devotions—English. 4. Junior
high school students—Prayer-books and devotions—English. I. Title.
BV283.S3F48   1997
242'.83—dc21   97-20174
                                                                          CIP

Contents

Introduction

The ideal of prayer as a part of everyday life goes back to Jesus of Nazareth, and even further than that, to the days of the ancient Israelites. Prayer as a part of the fabric of the ordinary is woven deeply into Christian tradition and everyday practice of the faith. If our Catholic faith is not a mere sideline or hobby, but the heart and soul of life itself, then prayer and a spirit of prayer belong smack in the midst of life itself.

The purpose of this collection of prayers and prayer services is to provide Catholic high schools with a resource to encourage a spirit of prayer in the context of ordinary, everyday life. The prayers connect with the liturgical calendar, the rich Catholic tradition of prayer for the intercession of the saints, school activities, the seasons of the year, and the ordinary lives of high school students in our society today.

In particular, this book was written with the classroom teacher and classroom circumstances in mind. The custom of beginning daily class time with prayer is one which, in some situations, could use some revitalization. This book provides teachers with a resource that is both practical and connected to the deepest and best in Catholic tradition.

The author of this book encourages both students and teachers to remember that we do not use prayers to make a situation holy, or to invoke God's presence in an otherwise profane setting. Rather, we use prayer to remind ourselves that the risen Christ is already with us, "wherever two or three are gathered in his name." It is in that awareness that these prayers are offered.

How to Use This Book

A few suggestions may make this book easier for you to use.

First, you may wonder how to pick a particular prayer for a particular day. Try the following strategy:

- First, check to see if any of the prayers in the third section, "Holy Days and Holidays" (p. 67) are appropriate. Is today a saint's day? Are you in the season of Advent or Lent?
- If none of these work, look at the second section, "Special Days" (p. 39). What is going on at your school today?
- If you still don't see anything that fits, turn to the first section, "Ordinary Days" (p. 9), and choose one of these.

On page 122, you will find a complete list of the prayers in this book. You may want to avoid repeating the same prayer too often—especially those in the first section. If so, you can use the chart given with this list to make note of the dates on which you use each prayer.

Finally, you may simply be looking for an easy way to introduce a prayer, to let everyone know that it's time to pray. If so, try one of the following phrases:

- "Let's pray together."
- "Let's pray together for _____ ."
- "Please join me in prayer."
- "Please join me in praying for _____."
- "Please pray with me."

ONE

Prayers for Ordinary Days

Prayers for Christian Character

An Everyday Prayer
To the Holy Spirit
For Faith
For Hope
For Love
For Joy
For Honesty
On Doing Our Best
About Drunk Driving
About Alcohol, Nicotine and Other
   Drugs
For Peace

Prayers for Christian Character

An Everyday Prayer

God our loving Father, today is an ordinary day like most
days. Yet this ordinary day is filled with your loving
kindness and your guiding Spirit. Thank you for the gift of
this day. Help us face difficult times with courage and
hope, and help us accept easy times with gratitude and
humility. Make us more aware of your love for us and the
joy you take in us as we go through this ordinary day. We
ask this in the name of Jesus, the Lord. Amen.

To the Holy Spirit

Come, Holy Spirit, fountain of eternal life, fill our hearts
with your love and inspire our minds with your wisdom.
Guide us by your light in the paths of truth, justice, peace,
and compassion. Give us the courage to ask questions and
the humility to recognize and accept truth, because only
the truth will make us free. Come, Holy Spirit, fill the
hearts of your people, and nourish us with your love. We
ask this in the name of Jesus, the Lord. Amen.

For Faith

Loving God, sometimes we struggle with the idea of faith and its meaning for us. Help us to be open to the gift of friendship with you and with Jesus, your Son, in the power and joy of your Holy Spirit. Show us that without faith, without friendship with you, our Creator, it is much easier for life to take wrong turns into darkness and unhappiness. Fill us with the gift of faith so that we may find life's deepest meaning and purpose and know your will for each one of us. We pray in the name of Jesus, the Lord. Amen.

For Hope

God our loving Father, sometimes it's hard to be hopeful. Help us to see that no matter how bleak things may seem at times, there is always the possibility of a better tomorrow. Help us to be hopeful about ourselves and our future, and help us to act on that hope by making good choices today. Fill us with hope for the future so we may rejoice in the gift of the present moment. We ask this in the name of Jesus, the Lord. Amen.

For Love

Your love for us has no limits, O God. Help us to feel the power and warmth of your love for us. Show us your love in all your creation and in our care and concern for one another. Teach us to act with genuine love and compassion in our interactions with one another. May we learn to love by reflecting on the life and teachings of Jesus, your Son, and may we reach out, in particular, to those who seem most difficult to love. We pray in the name of Jesus, the Lord. Amen.

For Joy

You take joy, O God, in all your creation and in all your people. We live in a society and culture that understands the idea of "fun" but rarely knows how to find genuine joy. Fill us with your Holy Spirit, loving God, so that we may know the joy that only you can give. Help us to find joy through loving service to those with special needs who may feel unloved, and help us to find joy, O God, above all through faith and trust in you. We pray in the name of Jesus, the Lord. Amen.

For Honesty

Loving God, help us to be honest in all that we do. We are sorry for the times when we have been less than completely honest. Give us the strength to be honest in our relationships with our teachers and with one another, to be honest when we take tests and when we do our homework, to be honest with our parents and with our employers. Above all, dear God, help us to be honest with ourselves. We ask this in the name of Jesus, the Lord. Amen.

On Doing Our Best

Loving God, you give each of us special gifts and you call each of us to serve you and one another in particular ways. Help us to do the very best we can in all that we do, in our studies and in our extracurricular activities. When we have opportunities to excel, encourage us toward excellence. When we feel like being lazy, remind us to fulfill our responsibilities. Help us, loving God, to always do our best at whatever we do. We pray in the name of Jesus, the Lord. Amen.

About Drunk Driving

Loving God, sometimes we forget what's good for us and what's not. We sometimes do things only because other people are doing them. If we find ourselves with other people who are using alcohol, help us to use good sense, O Lord, and get ourselves out of that situation. Give us the courage to do whatever we can to keep people who have been drinking from driving. Bless us with a spirit of common sense and inner strength, O God. We pray in the name of Jesus, the Lord. Amen.

About Alcohol, Nicotine and Other Drugs

God our loving Father, you create us with a capacity for joy that has no limits. Help us to remember that true joy and inner freedom do not come from the use of alcohol, nicotine and drugs, but from loving relationships, with you and with other people. When we feel sad, depressed, lonely, or frustrated, remind us to turn to you and to other people who can help us deal with our problems in positive ways. Help us prefer the true joy you give to the phony feelings that come from alcohol, nicotine and drugs. We pray in the name of Jesus, the Lord. Amen.

For Peace

Lord Jesus, following the mystery of your resurrection, you said to your disciples, "Peace I leave with you, my peace I give to you." Thank you for the gift of peace. Help us to work for peace in our daily lives, and help us to find peace by giving ourselves completely to you. Show us how to be people of peace. We pray in the name of Jesus, the Lord. Amen.

Prayers for Relationships

Prayers for Relationships

For Good Relationships

Lord Jesus, risen Christ, you teach us that we find life's deepest meaning when we cultivate healthy relationships with God and other people. Help us to be open to your presence in our lives, and help us to work at having good relationships with others, relationships based on honor, respect, and a desire to help others be their best selves. We ask for these gifts in your name. Amen.

For Parents and Family

God our loving Father, thank you for our parents and other family members. Sometimes family relationships are stressful and difficult. Other times we feel grateful for the ways our parents, guardians, and brothers and sisters enrich our lives. We understand that while friends are important, our families are for always. Thank you, O God, for our families, and help us to be patient with them. We pray in the name of Jesus, the Lord. Amen.

For Healing in Families

Loving God, sometimes we have a hard time getting along with one another in our families. Sometimes we feel angry with our parents and brothers or sisters, and they sometimes feel angry with us. Family relationships can be painful and difficult. Bring healing to our families, dear God, and help us to work through conflict and differences in constructive ways. Help us to remember that we do love one another. We pray in the name of Jesus, the Lord. Amen.

For Courtesy and Respect

God our loving Father, you live in each one of us.
Therefore, we all have an infinite dignity, and we are all
destined for union with you in this life and eternal
happiness with you in the next. Teach us to recognize you
in one another and to relate to one another with courtesy
and respect. May those who observe our school
community be inspired by our behavior to remark, "See
how they love one another." We ask this in the name of
Jesus, the Lord. Amen.

For Dating Relationships

Loving God, you reveal yourself to us in those we care
about. We give thanks especially for dating experiences.
Help us to open our dating relationships to your loving
presence, and help us always to honor, respect, and
appreciate one another as you honor, respect, and
appreciate each one of us. We pray in the name of Jesus,
the Lord. Amen.

On Making Good Choices
About Sexual Behavior

God our loving Creator, from you we receive the gift of our
sexuality. We thank you for this gift, and we ask you to
help us learn to use it with love and respect for ourselves
and one another. We live in a society that often trivializes
sex in movies, music, and the print media. Help us to
respect the gift of sex by saving it for marriage. We pray in
the name of Jesus, the Lord. Amen.

For Friends

Lord Jesus, you call us your friends. We thank you for the gift of all our friends. In their friendship we feel your love for us. Help us to be true friends, always ready to give as well as receive. Help us also to be friends to those who are lonely, both those in and outside of our school community. We pray in the name of Jesus, the Lord. Amen.

For Those Who Feel Lonely

Dear God, your Son, Jesus, felt lonely when all his friends abandoned him in the garden of Gethsemane. We pray for those who are lonely; help them to know that such feelings are temporary. Remind them that many people have the same feelings of loneliness. Help those who are lonely to turn to you, deep within themselves, so they may know how much you love them. Show us how to care for those who are lonely and reach out to them in friendship. We pray in the name of Jesus, the Lord. Amen.

On Eliminating Gossip

Loving God, you who are Truth, Love, and Forgiveness, help us to make no room for gossip. We know that gossip does no one any good. Gossip only hurts people who are not there to speak for themselves. Loving God, give us the self-discipline to avoid gossip. We pray in the name of Jesus, the Lord. Amen.

For Peace in Our School

O God who loves us more than we can ever imagine, we know that you want us to live in peace. You want us to live together in peace not only in the outside world, but here in our school where we spend so many hours together each week. Help us to work for peace by working to see that everyone is treated fairly. Teach us to respect one another and care for one another. We pray in the name of Jesus, the Lord. Amen.

For Equality

Loving God, in your eyes all people have infinite worth. You rejoice in the variety that exists among your people. You created female and male, many different races, nations, and cultures. Help us to work for equality in our school and in our world. May no one suffer rejection or prejudice because of race, gender, or social or economic status. May there be no room for "in groups" or "out groups." Instead, may all be accepted for the basic human dignity that is your gift, O God, to each and every one. We pray in the name of Jesus, the Lord. Amen.

Prayers for Those in Our School Community

For the Freshman Class

For the Sophomore Class

For the Junior Class

For the Senior Class

In Appreciation of Non-Conformists

For Those Struggling with Depression

For Anyone Thinking of Suicide

For Teachers

For Our Principal

For the Office Staff

For the Custodial Staff

For the Yearbook Staff

For the School Newspaper Staff

For Coaches

For Cheerleaders

For Athletic Opponents

For Referees

Prayers for Those in Our School Community

For the Freshman Class

Loving Father, you are the source of all new beginnings. We give thanks for our freshman class, and we ask you to be present to all those beginning high school this year. Help them to be not afraid but to embrace their high school years with courage, hope, and determination to do their best. Give to them a deep conviction of your love for them, and help them to take advantage of the opportunities that come their way. We pray in the name of Jesus, the Lord. Amen.

For the Sophomore Class

Loving God, the second year of high school sometimes feels "in-between"—no longer freshmen but still a long way from being seniors. Help our sophomore class to build on the good beginning they made as freshmen. Give them a spirit of quiet humility and joy with a heavy dose of courage, fortitude, and patience. Help the sophomore class to stay focused on their goals and continue to do their best in all that they do. We ask this in the name of Jesus, the Lord. Amen.

For the Junior Class

God our loving Father, we give you thanks for our junior class. Strengthen them during this, their third year of high school, as they take on more leadership roles in our school community and begin looking forward to their senior year and after-high school plans. Even with the future shining ahead of them, O God, help our junior class to remain focused on the joys and challenges of the present. We ask this in the name of Jesus, the Lord. Amen.

For the Senior Class

Loving God, we give you thanks for our senior class. We thank you for their many accomplishments over the past three years. Inspire them to dedicate themselves to an even more successful final year at our school. Help our seniors to fulfill their responsibilities and to enjoy the present, while maintaining a healthy perspective on the future. We pray in the name of Jesus, the Lord. Amen.

In Appreciation of Non-Conformists

God, you are like a loving and compassionate Mother to us, yet sometimes you are unpredictable. Sometimes you act in ways that don't conform to our expectations for you. We ask your blessing, then, on people who surprise us by the way they dress, their hair styles, or the music they listen to. They remind us that being like everyone else can sometimes keep us from good ideas and worthwhile adventures. Bless non-conformists, we pray. We ask this in the name of the ultimate non-conformist, Jesus, the Lord. Amen.

For Those Struggling with Depression

God our loving Father, sometimes a cloud of depression and discouragement hangs over us, and we don't know what to do about it. Everything seems difficult and nothing seems to make any difference in how we feel. Other people irritate us, and we find it hard to do our work and participate in our classes and other activities. Help those of us who feel depressed, O God. Bring healing, and give them the strength to ask for help. We pray in the name of Jesus, the Lord. Amen.

For Anyone Thinking of Suicide

Lord God, from you we receive the gift of life itself. But sometimes life can seem like a huge burden, and people can feel so depressed and hopeless that they think about taking their own life. We pray for anyone in our school who may have such feelings and thoughts. Help them to feel your overwhelming love for them, O God. Show them that suicide is a drastic and permanent way to deal with a temporary problem. Guide them to someone who can help. For anyone who may think of suicide, we pray in the name of Jesus, the Lord. Amen.

For Teachers

Loving God, Father, Son, and Holy Spirit, we thank you for the blessing of dedicated, generous, gifted teachers. We thank you for the many sacrifices our teachers make in order to teach in a Catholic school. Bless each one of our teachers, we pray. Fill them with your gift of wisdom. Give them lightness of heart, deep love for you, and joy in the work that they do. We pray in the name of Jesus, the Lord. Amen.

For Our Principal

God our loving Father, we offer a prayer for our principal, _____. Help him/her to be the kind of principal our school needs. Guide him/her in the paths of justice, wisdom, and compassion, and help him/her to have a joyful heart and a good sense of humor. We offer this prayer in the name of Jesus, the Lord. Amen.

For the Office Staff

Loving God, we thank you for the people who make up the staff of our school office. It would be impossible for our school to operate without them. Bless our office staff with a sense of humor, fingers that fly over the keyboards, and the gift of being in control in the midst of apparent chaos. We pray in the name of Jesus, the Lord. Amen.

For the Custodial Staff

God our loving Father, we thank you for our custodial staff. Our school would soon become a very unpleasant place without them. Help us to make their job easier by being neat, respecting school property, and cleaning up after ourselves. Bless our custodial staff and help them to be patient with us. We ask this in the name of Jesus, the Lord. Amen.

For the Yearbook Staff

God our loving Father, our school year is filled with so
many activities and events, so many memories. We thank
you for the hard work of our yearbook staff in keeping a
record for us of the memories and the people that make up
our academic year. Bless them, we pray—the writers,
editors, and photographers—for all their hard work. We
ask this in the name of Jesus, the Lord. Amen.

For the School Newspaper Staff

Loving God, we ask you to bless our school newspaper
staff. Keep their wits sharp, their pens and notebooks
ready, and their hearts prepared to seek the truth. May
their writing be lively and their cameras in focus. Help
them to write features that are interesting, editorials that
are thought-provoking, and news stories that inform and
educate. We pray in the name of Jesus, the Lord. Amen.

For Coaches

God our loving Father, we pray for our (*may give name of
sport*) coaches. We thank you for their unselfish dedication
to our athletic program. We thank you for all the hours
they give to working with our team(s) and for the honor
they bring to our school by their leadership and
commitment to athletic excellence. Lord God, we ask you
to bless our coaches. Help them to help us to be the best
that we can be. We pray in the name of Jesus, the Lord.
Amen.

For Cheerleaders

Loving God, in our cheerleaders we see your joy and enthusiasm for us and for everything in creation. Help our cheerleaders perform their routines with precision. Encourage the rest of us to support our teams. We thank you for our cheerleaders, and ask you to keep them safe and free from injuries today and all season long. We pray in the name of Jesus, the Lord. Amen.

For Athletic Opponents

God our loving Father, we thank you for all the other schools we compete against in sports. Without them there would be no game. Help us to respect our opponents and remember that they enjoy playing the game as much as we do. Bless our opponents with a desire to play fairly and observe the traditions of good sportsmanship. Regardless of who wins, may our opponents have a good experience playing against us. We pray in the name of Jesus, the Lord. Amen.

For Referees

God of truth and justice, we pray for our referees whose task it is to help us play fairly and according to the rules. Help their eyes to be sharp, their calls to be accurate, and their ears deaf to insults. Remind us to behave toward our referees with honor and respect. We pray in the name of Jesus, the Lord. Amen.

Prayers for World Concerns

For Peace in the World

For Reconciliation
  Between Peoples at War

For the United States of America

For All People

For the Environment

For Those Who Are Hungry

For Those Who Are Poor

For Racial Unity and Peace

For Peace in Our Neighborhoods

Prayers for World Concerns

For Peace in the World

Lord Jesus, you said to your disciples, "Blessed are the peacemakers, for they will be called children of God." You know how much our world needs your gift of peace, yet in so many places there is only war and conflict. Today we pray especially for the conflict in _name a place_. Lord, through the power of your Holy Spirit, transform human hearts, give our world a desire for peace, and help us to do our part. We pray in your holy name. Amen.

For Reconciliation Between Peoples at War

Loving God, war destroys people's lives. It is an expression of despair, a last resort, a dependence on violence to settle differences and disagreements. God of peace, help those who are at war to long for peace. Help those who want peace to long for justice for all concerned, so that peace may become possible. Banish war from our world, O God. We pray in the name of Jesus, the Lord. Amen.

For the United States of America

God our loving Father, we pray for our country, the United States of America. We thank you for the many freedoms we enjoy; keep us mindful of the countless peoples of the earth who are not free. We thank you for our many material benefits; keep us mindful of the countless peoples of the earth, even in our own country, who live with hunger and poverty. Bless our leaders with a wisdom that transcends party politics, and help us all to contribute to the life of our nation in ways that will benefit others. We pray in the name of Jesus, the Lord. Amen.

For All People

Lord God, Creator of the universe, you have no favorites among the nations of the earth. All peoples are your children. Different cultures and religions call you by different names, yet all sense your holy presence. We pray for the other countries with whom we share your world. Bless them, Lord God. Help them to enjoy freedom and prosperity, and help us to be generous to other countries when they need our help. We pray in the name of Jesus, the Lord. Amen.

For the Environment

God our loving Creator, you bring us into being as a part of nature, and you give us our natural environment in which to make a home. From you come the gifts of oceans, rivers and lakes, trees, and air to breathe. Help us to do all that we can to preserve our natural environment as we do our work, live in our homes, and create means of transportation. Bless the earth and sky, loving God, and help us to use all our natural resources with future generations in mind. We pray in the name of Jesus, the Lord. Amen.

For Those Who Are Hungry

Lord Jesus, you showed concern for a large crowd of people when they followed you into a remote place and were hungry. You fed all the people with two fish and five loaves of bread. In our world, in our country, in our own community, many people live with hunger every day. Yet there is more than enough in our world to feed everyone. Help the nations of the earth learn to share, Lord Jesus, so that no one has to go hungry. Bless those who do not have enough to eat today. Show us what we have to do to make sure everyone has enough food. We pray through the intercession of the Holy Spirit and in your holy name. Amen.

For Those Who Are Poor

God our loving Father, in his life on earth your Son Jesus showed a particular care and concern for those who were poor. Compared to the overwhelming majority of the people in the world, we have so much. Bless those who are poor, Lord God. Give them strength and courage, and keep us mindful of them in all that we do. Help us to care for those who have less than we do, both in distant places and in our own community. Teach us to be generous in sharing of our time and money. We pray in the name of Jesus, the Lord. Amen.

For Racial Unity and Peace

Loving God, you created your people in a wonderful variety of races and cultures. Help us to empty our hearts of any traces of racial prejudice. Help all your people to be at peace with one another in the many-colored quilt of society. We pray in the name of Jesus, the Lord. Amen.

For Peace in Our Neighborhoods

God our loving Father, you want all your people to live in peace. Yet our neighborhoods are sometimes not so peaceful. Help us to work for peace and justice close to our homes so that our neighborhoods may be safe. We pray in the name of Jesus, the Lord. Amen.

TWO

Prayers for Special Days

Prayers on Fridays

For a Good Weekend
For Weekend Parties

Prayers on Fridays

For a Good Weekend

Thank you, God our Father, for the gift of this weekend. Show us how to use our weekend in ways that will help us to feel good about ourselves. Should we find ourselves in situations where we are tempted to join activities that we know are unhealthy or dangerous, give us the courage to leave those situations as quickly as possible regardless of what others may say or think. Loving God, help us to relax this weekend in ways that will bring true physical, emotional, and spiritual refreshment, and help us find time to do our homework well. We ask this in the name of Jesus, the Lord. Amen.

For Weekend Parties

Lord Jesus, this weekend there will be parties at various places. We thank you for the freedom to get together, to relax, and to enjoy one another's company. Give us the courage and common sense to keep alcohol and drugs away from our parties. Help us refuse to let nicotine pollute our bodies, which are dwelling places for your Holy Spirit. Make our parties a good experience for everyone. We pray in your name. Amen.

Prayers for
School Activities

For School Elections
For Open House
For a School Play
For a Concert
For an Art Show

Prayers for School Activities

For School Elections

Loving God, we ask you to bless those who are running for various offices in student government. Help everyone to run a fair campaign with a good spirit, and help everyone to vote for the people who seem best qualified for the office they seek. Give those who win a sense of dedication to serving others, and help those who lose to do so with grace. We pray in the name of Jesus, the Lord. Amen.

For Open House

God our loving Father, today we welcome visitors to our school from the wider community in which we live. Help us to show them a spirit of hospitality permeated by the warmth and joy of your Spirit. Help us to see you in each visitor, and may their time here be one they will always cherish. We ask this in the name of Jesus, the Lord. Amen.

For a School Play

Loving God, the cast and crew of our play have spent many long hours in preparation and rehearsal. We thank you for their dedication and commitment to a quality production. Give everyone involved a sense of calmness and confidence, and may each person who stands in the spotlight reflect you. We pray in the name of Jesus, the Lord. Amen.

For a Concert

God of life, we praise your vibrant and exciting Spirit which fills the universe. Music, especially, reminds us of the vitality and power of your Spirit. Help our musicians to play well for the concert, and give everyone a sense of your presence in the music and their talents as we listen. We ask this in the name of Jesus, the Lord. Amen.

For an Art Show

Loving God, when you created the earth and the whole universe you revealed yourself to us in ways we can see, taste, touch, hear and feel. We praise you in all of creation. When we create works of art we imitate you, our Creator. Let our art show give honor to your creativity at work in us, and may all the works of art draw people closer to the Good, True, and Beautiful which is at the heart of all creation. We pray in the name of Jesus, the Lord. Amen.

Prayers for Academic Occasions

For Freshman Orientation
To Welcome New Students
For Those Taking S.A.T.s / A.C.T.s
For Report Card Time
For Final Exams

Prayers for Academic Occasions

For Freshmen Orientation

On this day of freshmen orientation we ask you to come, Holy Spirit, and guide our freshmen as they get to know a new school, new teachers, new classes, and new friends. Fill them with openness to the future with all the unknowns that it holds and remind them that what the future holds most of all is your divine love. On orientation day we ask you to bless our new freshmen with a sense of direction, a relaxed feeling about meeting new people, and a readiness to embrace the challenge of high school with confidence and enthusiasm. We pray in the name of Jesus, the Lord. Amen.

To Welcome New Students

God our loving Father, we ask you to bless our new students and help them to feel welcome and a part of our school community. Remind students and teachers who are "old timers" to be helpful and courteous to our new students. At the same time, help our newcomers to find their way around and adapt to their new classes easily. Bless them with many friends and much success in all that they do. We pray in the name of Jesus, the Lord. Amen.

For Those Taking S.A.T.s / A.C.T.s

Loving God, there is a lot of pressure when it comes to taking S.A.T.s and A.C.T.s. Help us to deal with the pressure by putting these tests in perspective. Help us to do our best, but help us to realize, too, that the most important test in life is not academic but personal and spiritual, the test of how well we love God and other people. Help us to have a clear mind as we take our tests. We ask this in the name of Jesus, the Lord. Amen.

For Report Card Time

Loving God, at report card time we know we can depend upon you to celebrate our successes with us and comfort us when we don't do so well. Help us to see our good grades as a reward for hard work and our not-so-good grades as an inspiration to double our efforts and work harder where more work is needed. Remind us to ask for help when we need it, and help us to rejoice that your love for us is always there, no matter what our grades may be. We pray in the name of Jesus, the Lord. Amen.

For Final Exams

Come Holy Spirit, fill us with desire and strength to study well for final exams. We give thanks for the gift of our education. Give us the will to learn and the humility to ask for help when we need it. When we sit down to take an exam help our minds to be clear, our memory strong, and our fingers free from writer's cramp. Bless our efforts during final exams. We pray in the name of Jesus, the Lord. Amen.

Prayers for
Social Occasions

For Homecoming

For a Dance

For a Prom

Prayers for Social Occasions

For Homecoming

Oh Lord, you rejoice when we take time to celebrate and enjoy our friends. We pray that you will come and bless our Homecoming festivities with your love. May our dance reflect the joy you find in us and in all of your creation. May our game reflect your own enthusiasm for living, and may the weather be conducive to joyful celebration. We pray in the name of Jesus, the Lord. Amen.

For a Dance

God of the dance, you created the whole universe as one big celebration. We pray that you will be with us as we celebrate at our dance. We thank you for the gifts of music and movement, and we pray that you will help us to act in ways that honor you and each other. Help us to stay close to you in all that we do. We ask this in the name of Jesus, the Lord. Amen.

For a Prom

Gracious God, we ask your blessing on our prom. May the music remind us of your creation of stars and planets spinning through space. May our formal dresses and tuxes remind us of the dignity and beauty we are clothed with as your daughters and sons. Bless our night together with a spirit of joy and mutual respect. We pray in the name of Jesus, the Lord. Amen.

Prayers for
Athletic Occasions

For Athletic Tryouts

Before the First Game of the Season

For a Safe Journey to an Away Game

For Fans Traveling to a Game

Before a Game with a Big Rival

For a Championship Game

At the End of the Season

Prayers for Athletic Occasions

For Athletic Tryouts

God of play, we thank you for the opportunity of athletics. We pray for the tryouts for the (*name of sport*) team. We ask your blessing on those who make the team and those who don't. Help those who make the team to be present for all the practices and play their best. Help those who do not make the team to find what they do best and to dedicate themselves to it with a full heart. We pray in the name of Jesus, the Lord. Amen.

Before the First Game of the Season

God our Father, we thank you for the joy of a new (*name of sport*) season. We thank you for strong, healthy bodies that enable us to play and compete. Before this first game of the season, we ask you to help our team and our opponents to remain injury-free. Help us to do our best. We ask this in the name of Jesus, the Lord. Amen.

For a Safe Journey to an Away Game

Loving God, as we begin our journey to our game at (*name of school*), we ask your blessing on our team, coaches, and driver(s). Help the road conditions to remain safe, help our driver(s) to remain alert, and help all of us make this a pleasant journey for everyone. We pray in the name of Jesus, the Lord. Amen.

For Fans Traveling to a Game

Loving God, help all fans who will be traveling to the game at (*name of school*) to arrive safely. Help them to enjoy the game, cheer on their favorite team, and be gracious in either victory or defeat. Help all the fans to a safe trip home. We pray in the name of Jesus, the Lord. Amen.

Before a Game with a Big Rival

Loving God, as we prepare for our game with (*name of school*), we ask your blessing on both teams. We enjoy competing when both teams have an intense desire to win. But we ask you, loving God, to remind us to keep our rivalry in perspective. Help us to rededicate ourselves to fair play and good sportsmanship. Give us the joy of your Spirit. We pray in the name of Jesus, the Lord. Amen.

For a Championship Game

Loving God, we thank you for bringing us to the point where we are able to play in a championship game. We thank you for giving us the physical and spiritual strength and stamina to get this far. We thank you for the talents and dedication of all our players. As we go into this championship game, help us to use all the gifts you have given us with enthusiasm and skill. Help us to give it our all. We pray in the name of Jesus, the Lord. Amen.

At the End of the Season

God of games and play, we thank you for the (*name of sport*) season that is coming to an end. We thank you for the efforts and enthusiasm of all the players, coaches, referees, and support personnel. Help us to recall this season as a time when both victory and defeat brought us closer to one another and to you. We pray in the name of Jesus, the Lord. Amen.

Prayers on
Difficult Occasions

On the Death of a Classmate
On the Death of a Family Member
At a Time When Many Are Sick
For an End to Gang Violence

Prayers on Difficult Occasions

On the Death of a Classmate

Lord Jesus, when your friend Lazarus died you wept and were deeply troubled in spirit. One of our friends and classmates has died, O Lord, and we are confused and sad. Be with us in our grief, and help us to trust in your love for (*name*) and for us. Help us to know in our hearts that on the other side of the mystery of death you are with us, even as you are with us in this life. Comfort us, and comfort (name)'s family and closest friends. Bring healing to us all, and help us to move ahead in our lives, in peace and in hope. We pray through the intercession of the Holy Spirit and in your holy name. Amen.

On the Death of a Family Member

Lord Jesus, today we remember (*give name of deceased*), the (*relation to student*) of (*give name of student*). We stand before the mystery of death with sorrow in our hearts. We don't understand. But we also believe that you are with us in our sorrow. You experienced what it means to be human even to sharing in the death that comes to us all. Be especially with (name of student) at this time of grieving, comfort others who are touched by this loss, and give us all a sense of trust and hope. We pray through the intercession of the Holy Spirit and in your holy name. Amen.

At a Time When Many Are Sick

Loving God, many people are sick these days. An illness is going around, and many are home in bed, miserable, unhappy, and missing out on what's going on in school. Some are falling behind in their school work. It's a bad situation all around. Help those who are sick to get well and return to school soon. While they are sick, comfort them and help them to be aware of your loving presence. We pray in the name of Jesus, the Lord. Amen.

For an End to Gang Violence

God our loving Father, sometimes it seems like violence is out of control. Our city streets have become dangerous places. Help the leaders of our city, state, and country to recognize the causes of gang violence and work to prevent it. Give gang members the courage to break the cycle of violence. Bring peace to our streets, O Lord. We pray in the name of Jesus, the Lord. Amen.

THREE

Prayers for Holy Days and Holidays

Prayers Through the Church Year

First Week of Advent

Second Week of Advent

Third Week of Advent

Fourth Week of Advent

Before Christmas Vacation

Ash Wednesday

First Week of Lent

Second Week of Lent

Third Week of Lent

Fourth Week of Lent

Fifth Week of Lent

Sixth Week of Lent

Holy Thursday

Good Friday

Before Easter Break

Ascension of the Lord

Pentecost

Prayers Through the Church Year

First Week of Advent

Loving God, this week we begin looking ahead with hope to our celebration of the birth of your Son who came among us as a helpless infant. Show us how to make Advent more than a commercial season of shopping, more than a time to look forward to what we will get. Help us to make of this Advent season a time to remember you, a time to give to those who have less than we. We pray in the name of Jesus, the Lord. Amen.

Second Week of Advent

God of Advent joy, our world is filled with reminders of a commercialized Christmas. Yet the lights and brightly decorated trees remind us also of the true Light that we look forward to during Advent. Help us to remember that Advent is an important time of preparation, a time to wait quietly as we look forward to celebrating the birth of Jesus. We pray in the name of Jesus, the Lord. Amen.

Third Week of Advent

Loving God of Advent, in these last weeks before Christmas we find you in our hope and expectation. We find in you the joy of anticipation. Help us to prepare ourselves for the celebration of your birth by caring for those who are less fortunate. We pray in the name of Jesus, the Lord. Amen.

Fourth Week of Advent

Lord Jesus, during this final week of Advent we find Christmas decorations, bright lights and the music of the season all around us. We enjoy parties and gift-giving, but remind us that what we celebrate above all is the festival of your birth into our world. As we approach the joy of Christmas, help us to think more of giving than receiving. We pray in the name of Jesus, the Lord. Amen.

Before Christmas Vacation

Lord Jesus, we look forward with excitement and anticipation to the celebration of your birth. In honor of your coming into our world and sharing our humanity, we have Christmas vacation, days for leisure, relaxation, and time with family and friends. Help us to have a joyous vacation and return to school renewed in mind, body, and spirit. We pray in your Holy Spirit and in your holy name. Amen.

Ash Wednesday

God our Father, your love for us has no limits. Your love surrounds us and supports us at all times and in all places. On Ash Wednesday we begin the holy season of Lent. Today we receive blessed ashes traced on our forehead in the shape of a cross. Help this ritual to remind us that life has no meaning apart from a deep dedication to loving you and serving one another. Help us to overcome selfishness and grow in generosity. We pray in the name of Jesus, the Lord. Amen.

First Week of Lent

Loving God, you give us the gift of Lent that we might recall how deep your love is for us. During this first week of Lent, help us to let go of habits and behaviors that are self-destructive. Strengthen our understanding of one another and our compassion for those who suffer rejection and cruelty. Help us to reach out in kindness to those who are unhappy. We pray in the name of Jesus, the Lord. Amen.

Second Week of Lent

God our loving Father, Lent is a time to become less centered on ourselves and more centered on others. During this second week of Lent, help us to find a few minutes in each day to pause and be aware of your presence in our lives, in our school, and in our world. Help us to make one daily extra effort to encourage someone who may feel discouraged, or include someone who may feel lonely. We pray in the name of Jesus, the Lord. Amen.

Third Week of Lent

Lord Jesus, you call us to a deep change of heart. During Lent we focus on your invitation to turn away from superficial values and self-destructive behaviors. You call us to accept abundant life and a joy that only you can give. Help us to open our hearts to the presence of your Spirit. We pray in your holy name. Amen.

Fourth Week of Lent

God our loving Father, sometimes we find it difficult to be hopeful. Sometimes life can be so discouraging. During Lent, remind us to turn to you and to one another to find a deeper hope and a deeper joy. Help us to see that no matter how hard life may seem, there are always people who want to help. Help us to see that, above all, you want to fill our hearts with a peace that no one else can give. We pray in the name of Jesus, the Lord. Amen.

Fifth Week of Lent

Loving God, you wait for us in every moment and every experience of our day. As Lent progresses, make us more aware of your unconditional love for us. Help us to be more vulnerable to one another, more open to one another's needs, and more open to your gift of yourself to us. We open our hearts to you. Remind us to trust you, especially when we are fearful. We pray in the name of Jesus, the Lord. Amen.

Sixth Week of Lent

God our loving Father, during this last week of Lent we thank you for your many blessings. We thank you for allowing us to become less centered on self and more open to the needs and concerns of others. Help us now to become more open to life and more eager for living. Help us to prepare ourselves to celebrate the resurrection of your Son, Jesus. We pray in his name. Amen.

Holy Thursday

Lord Jesus, we remember your gift of your whole self—body and blood, soul and divinity—to your people at the Last Supper. In the eucharist you nourish us as we dedicate ourselves over and over to a life based on love of God and neighbor. Deepen our appreciation and respect for this great sacrament, Lord Jesus. We pray in your holy name and in your Holy Spirit. Amen.

Good Friday

Lord Jesus, we remember your death on the cross. Because of your love for us, you accepted a deeply painful and unjust death. You could have escaped death, but you wanted to share fully in all that it means to be human, even the death that we all must pass through. You wanted to save us. We thank you for drinking the cup of human existence to the last drop. Help us, in and through your Holy Spirit, to do the same. We pray in your holy name. Amen.

Before Easter Break

Lord Jesus, at the beginning of our Easter break we thank you for the joy of your resurrection which our time away from school celebrates. Help us to have a safe, renewing Easter break so we may return to school refreshed and rested. Fill each one of us with your power of new life. We pray in your Holy Spirit and in your holy name. Amen.

Ascension of the Lord

Lord Jesus, today we celebrate your return to the Father in heaven. Help us to remember that, like you, this earth is not our final home, that we are destined to be with you sharing eternal life and eternal joy. Help us to make our choices in this life in the light of our ultimate destiny with you. We pray in your Holy Spirit and in your holy name. Amen.

Pentecost

Lord Jesus, this Sunday we will celebrate your gift of the Holy Spirit to your first disciples and to us. Fill us with the strength and courage of Pentecost. May your Holy Spirit bring us an abundance of wisdom and common sense. We pray in your Holy Spirit and in your holy name. Amen.

Prayers for Holidays

Prayers for Holidays

Feast of the Assumption (August 15)

Gracious God, at the end of her earthly life, you raised the Blessed Virgin Mary, body and soul, to live in eternal glory with you. Help us remember that like Mary, we too are called, body and soul, to live eternally with you. Thank you for the gift of our human nature, for our souls and our bodies. We pray in your Holy Spirit and in your holy name. Amen.

First Day of Autumn

Loving God, we thank you for the variety of the seasons. As autumn begins we look forward to the evening of the year. We appreciate again the beautiful fall colors you send. We thank you for the summer that is ending, and we welcome the cooler days ahead. This autumn, remind us of your love which is always appearing in new ways. We pray in the name of Jesus, the Lord. Amen.

Columbus Day

Loving God, today we observe Columbus Day. Help us to recall Christopher Columbus' spirit of adventure and his willingness to take risks in order to follow his dream. Give us the courage to follow our dreams and to be willing to take chances for the sake of new possibilities. Remind us also that our plans and projects should never disrespect or hurt others. We pray in the name of Jesus, the Lord. Amen.

Halloween

Loving God, today we celebrate Halloween, the eve of All Saints Day, with costumes, fun and laughter. Children come to our doors for "trick-or-treat," and we celebrate with Halloween parties, candy and other treats. Help us to enjoy the fun of Halloween as a sign of your playful Spirit. We pray in the name of Jesus, the Lord. Amen.

Feast of All Saints (November 1)

All the saints of heaven, today we celebrate your feast day. Your example of faithfulness to the gospel inspires us to rely on your prayers. We remember our own participation in the communion of saints that is present in this world and in eternity. Help us by your prayers to remain faithful to Christ during our earthly pilgrimage. We pray in the name of Jesus, the Lord. Amen.

Feast of All Souls (November 2)

Loving God, today we celebrate our relationship with all people in this life and in eternity. We thank you for this community that transcends space and time. May the prayers of those we love who now enjoy eternal light help us on our way. We pray in the name of Jesus, the Lord. Amen.

Election Day

God of truth and justice, today our nation votes for our representatives in government and decides on proposals for new legislation. We ask you to guide the hearts and minds of all voters. Help our nation to vote in a spirit of truth, justice, and compassion. We pray in the name of Jesus, the Lord. Amen.

Veterans Day

Loving God, today we remember all those who have served in our country's military service. Bless those who have made special sacrifices, including those who have fought in wars. In the future help our country to exhaust all other options before resorting to military force. We pray in the name of Jesus, the Lord. Amen.

Before Thanksgiving Break

Loving God, you are the source of all things good in our lives. As we begin our Thanksgiving break, help us to reflect on all your blessings and be thankful for them. We thank you for a few days for rest and relaxation. Help us to use our time wisely and well, and return to school refreshed and ready to work again. We pray in the name of Jesus, the Lord. Amen.

Feast of the Immaculate Conception (December 8)

Lord Jesus, today we recall the church's belief that your Blessed Mother was free from all sin from the moment of her conception. Remind us that in our lives, too, the grace of God is always more powerful than sin and guilt. Help us to be open to this grace. We pray in your Holy Spirit and in your holy name. Amen.

First Day of Winter

Loving God, we thank you for the gift of the seasons. As autumn gives way to winter we thank you for this time when the earth sleeps and waits. Help us to enjoy the changes this season brings. Keep us mindful, also, of those who may find it difficult to stay warm or get enough to eat this winter. We pray in the name of Jesus, the Lord. Amen.

Martin Luther King Day

Loving God, your servant Martin Luther King, Jr. stood for justice for all people. He dedicated his life to justice while rejecting violence in all its forms. Help us to be inspired by his example, and help us to follow it in our attitudes toward racial equality and social justice. We pray in the name of Jesus, the Lord. Amen.

Valentine's Day

Oh God, you create us out of your passionate love. On this day that celebrates romantic love, help us to recall that in romantic love we find a hint of your unconditional love for us. May the prayers of Saint Valentine help us to love you and our neighbors in all the ways you call us to. We pray in the name of Jesus, the Lord. Amen.

First Day of Spring

God of new life, we thank you for the gift of spring. May this season remind us that new life is always possible even when things seem most bleak and lifeless. As the earth is reborn, help us to remember that we, too, are reborn through faith. May the flowers and newly green trees be a constant reminder of your love for us. We pray in the name of Jesus, the Lord. Amen.

April Fool's Day

Sometimes, Lord God, you act in unexpected ways. Your creation is filled with surprising, amazing, sometimes outrageous things. Thank you for your sense of humor. Help us remember today that laughter and jokes that don't hurt anyone are a reminder of your creative sense of humor and play. May we recall, too, that you invite all of us to become fools for the sake of Christ, to be out of step in ways that bring more joy and love to the world. We pray in the name of Jesus, the Lord. Amen.

May Day: Month Dedicated to Mary the Mother of Jesus

Blessed Mother Mary, during this month dedicated to you may we always recall that you show us the motherly love of God. When we see the image of you and your Son, Madonna and Child, may we remember that this is also an image of God's love for us. Pray for us, that we may know that God loves each one of us with a love that is even far greater than the love of a mother for her child. And when we die, Blessed Mary, pray for us that we may be forever with you and your Son, Jesus, in heaven. We pray in his name. Amen.

Mother's Day

Loving God, you are like a Father and a Mother to us. This Sunday we will celebrate Mother's Day. We thank you for our mothers, who have loved us and cared for us. We pray for our mothers, whether they are still with us in this world or with you now in eternity. Bless them abundantly, O God, and help them to be patient with themselves and with us. We pray in the name of Jesus, the Lord. Amen.

Memorial Day

God our loving Creator, today we prayerfully remember all those who have given their lives in military service for our country. We thank you for their willingness to sacrifice for others. Show us what sacrifices we might make to make our nation a better place for all its citizens. We pray in the name of Jesus, the Lord. Amen.

Prayers for Saints' Days

Birth of the Virgin Mary (September 8)
Saint Peter Claver (September 9)
The Guardian Angels (October 2)
Saint Francis of Assisi (October 4)
Our Lady of the Rosary (October 7)
Saint Frances Xavier Cabrini (November 13)
Saint Elizabeth of Hungary (November 17)
Our Lady of Guadalupe (December 12)
Saint John of the Cross (December 14)
Saint Francis de Sales (January 24)
Saint Thomas Aquinas (January 28)
Saint John Bosco (January 31)
Saint Scholastica (February 10)
Our Lady of Lourdes (February 11)
Saint Patrick (March 17)
Saint Joseph (March 19)
Annunciation of the Lord (March 25)
Saint Catherine of Siena (April 29)
Saint Joseph the Worker (May 1)
Saint Mary Magdalene (May 25)
Saint Anthony of Padua (June 13)

Prayers for Saints' Days

Birth of the Virgin Mary (September 8)

Loving God, today we celebrate the birthday of the mother of your Son, Jesus. When Mary was born, the time of our salvation neared. Help us, O God, through the prayers of the Blessed Virgin Mary, to be open to your will in our lives as she was open to your will in her life. Holy Mary, Mother of God, pray for us. Amen.

Saint Peter Claver (September 9)

Loving God, in early 17th-century Spain your servant Peter Claver became a Jesuit and left his homeland forever to be a missionary in Columbia, South America. There he spent his life caring for Africans sold into slavery. Help us, O God, through the prayers of Peter Claver, to have active compassion for the "outcasts" of our own time. Saint Peter Claver, pray for us. Amen.

The Guardian Angels (October 2)

Loving God, your marvelous creation includes beings of pure spirit called angels. Tradition tells us that each of us has a guardian angel to watch over and guide us. By devotion to our guardian angel we express our faith in your enduring love, O God, and your constant care for us day after day, until life's end. Guardian angels, nurture and guide us by your prayers. Amen.

Saint Francis of Assisi (October 4)

Loving God, when he was young many people called your servant Francis crazy because he took his faith and your love for all of creation so much to heart. Francis felt your love so deeply that he was ready to sacrifice everything for that love. Through the prayers of Francis, O God, help us to love you and your creation as deeply as he did. Saint Francis of Assisi, pray for us. Amen.

Our Lady of the Rosary (October 7)

Loving God, we thank you for Our Lady of the Rosary. Our devotion to her helps us to meditate on the life of your Son. Through the prayers of Mary, O God, help us to be more prayerful people. Our Lady of the Rosary, pray for us. Amen.

Saint Frances Xavier Cabrini (November 13)

Loving God, thank you for Frances Xavier Cabrini, the first citizen of the United States to be canonized a saint. Mother Cabrini's deep trust in your love gave her the strength to carry out the work of your Son in spite of discouragement and difficulties at every step. Through the prayers of Frances Xavier Cabrini, O God, help us to follow her example by caring for the poor and downtrodden of our own time. Saint Frances Xavier Cabrini, pray for us. Amen.

Saint Elizabeth of Hungary (November 17)

Loving God, thank you for your servant Elizabeth, the daughter of the king of Hungary. A happily married woman, Elizabeth showed such a great love for the poor and suffering that she became the patron saint of Catholic charities. Through the prayers of Elizabeth, O God, help us to follow her example by an active love for those less fortunate than ourselves. Saint Elizabeth of Hungary, pray for us. Amen.

Our Lady of Guadalupe (December 12)

Loving God, we remember your servant Juan Diego, a poor man who lived in a village near Mexico City in the 16th century and who received visits from the Blessed Virgin Mary. She appeared to him as a young Native American maiden and spoke to him in his own language. As a sign of her love for all peoples, the famous image of Our Lady of Guadalupe appeared on the cape, or tilma, worn by Blessed Juan Diego. Through the prayers of Our Lady of Guadalupe, O God, help us to remember that your love for the poor is constant. Our Lady of Guadalupe, pray for us. Amen.

Saint John of the Cross (December 14)

Loving God, we remember your servant John, who helped to reform the Carmelite order in the 16th century and spent many months in prison for his efforts. He also wrote great works of mystical theology and poetry. Through the prayers of Saint John of the Cross, O God, help us to see the positive value of self-denial and discipline for the sake of love. Saint John of the Cross, pray for us. Amen.

Saint Francis de Sales (January 24)

Loving God, we recall your servant Francis de Sales, who went against his father's wishes and became a priest. His writings on the meaning of a Christian life in the everyday world remain classics today. Following Francis's example, O God, may we each welcome your special calling. St. Francis de Sales, pray for us. Amen.

Saint Thomas Aquinas (January 28)

Loving God, we remember your servant Thomas Aquinas, who rejected his parents' plans for him and became a Dominican friar. Even when his mother had him kidnapped and held at home against his will, he remained faithful to his vocation and later became the greatest Catholic theologian of all time. Help us, O God, to follow Thomas' example and use for good the intellectual abilities you give us. St. Thomas Aquinas, pray for us. Amen.

Saint John Bosco (January 31)

Loving God, we recall that in the mid-19th century your servant John Bosco promoted a theory of education based on love and respect for the individual student. John encouraged frequent reception of the sacraments of eucharist and reconciliation. He cared for and educated poor youths, and founded the Salesian Fathers and Sisters to serve poor boys and girls. Help us, O God, to follow John's example by sharing with those who have less. St. John Bosco, pray for us. Amen.

Saint Scholastica (February 10)

Loving God, we remember your servant Scholastica, the twin sister of Saint Benedict. Scholastica dedicated her life entirely to the love of you and then discovered that her love for you increased her love for other people. Help us, O God, to be inspired by Scholastica's example to love you with our whole heart, mind, and soul, and our neighbor as ourselves. Saint Scholastica, pray for us. Amen.

Our Lady of Lourdes (February 11)

Loving God, we thank you for your Blessed Mother's appearance to a French peasant girl, Bernadette Soubirous, in 1858, at Lourdes, France. Through her appearances to Bernadette, Mary revitalized the faith of millions, and to this day countless people visit her shrine at Lourdes. Through the prayers of your Blessed Mother, O God, give new life to our faith, as well. Our Lady of Lourdes, pray for us. Amen.

Saint Patrick (March 17)

Loving God, your servant Patrick brought the Christian faith to the people of Ireland in the 5th century. Through Patrick's prayers, O God, drive from our hearts all that comes between us and yourself, as Patrick once drove all the snakes from Ireland. On this day when we wear green to remind us of Ireland, St. Patrick, pray for us. Amen.

Saint Joseph (March 19)

Loving God, you chose Joseph to be the husband of Mary and to be the one to serve as your Son's foster father in this world. Joseph was completely open to all that God wanted him to do. He was a risk-taker and a man of deep faith. Through Joseph's prayers, O God, help us to seek and follow your will. St. Joseph, pray for us. Amen.

Annunciation of the Lord (March 25)

Loving God, today we celebrate that through the free choice of Mary, your Son was able to become a human being like us in all things except sin. Mary's "yes" opened the door to our salvation. May her prayers help us, O God, be channels of your love in our world. Holy Mary, Mother of God, pray for us. Amen.

Saint Catherine of Siena (April 29)

Loving God, today we remember Saint Catherine of Siena, a doctor of the church. Catherine always encouraged people to be patient with themselves, reminding us that becoming a faithful follower of Christ takes a lifetime. Help us, O God, through the prayers of Catherine of Siena, to be patient with ourselves. St. Catherine of Siena, pray for us. Amen.

Saint Joseph the Worker (May 1)

Loving God, you entrusted your Son to the care of Joseph who no doubt taught him to work at his trade as a carpenter. Remind us, O God, that whether we build a table and chair, an automobile or a computer program, we are called to do good things with hands and mind in order to prepare for the coming of your kingdom. Saint Joseph the Worker, pray for us. Amen.

Saint Mary Magdalene de Pazzi (May 25)

Loving God, in late 16th-century Italy you gave Mary Magdalene de Pazzi special gifts of loving intimacy with you, along with many difficulties and much suffering. Through it all, she remained hopeful and more concerned with others than with herself. Help us, O God, through the prayers of Mary Magdalene de Pazzi, not to let success make us think ourselves superior to others, and not to let difficulties or failure get us down. Saint Mary Magdalene de Pazzi, pray for us. Amen.

Saint Anthony of Padua (June 13)

Loving God, in early 13th century Italy you called your servant Anthony of Padua to the Franciscan Order where he became a man of deep prayer and a great scholar of theology and scripture. Anthony found himself by giving himself entirely to you. Following his death, popular devotion called Anthony the finder of lost objects. Help us, O God, through the prayers of Anthony, to find ourselves by giving ourselves to you. Saint Anthony of Padua, pray for us. Amen.

FOUR

Prayer Services for Various Occasions

Prayer Services for Various Occasions

The emphasis in the following prayer services is on simplicity and brevity. Few materials are needed, and a bare minimum of preparation is required. In other words, the busy schedules of both teachers and students are taken into account.

For Beginning the School Year

For Reconciliation

For the Beginning of Lent (Ash Wednesday)

To Remember the Last Supper

To Remember Christ's Passion

For the End of the School Year

Prayer Service for Beginning the School Year

This prayer service may be used with a large group, e.g. the entire student body, but is perhaps better suited to smaller groups in a classroom setting—during homeroom period, for example. Prior to this prayer service, ask several students to compose specific prayers of petition suitable for the beginning of a new school year.

Materials needed: candle, recorded music. The recorded music may be anything, instrumental or vocal—"secular" or "sacred"—that is appropriate to a meditative mood. A familiar classical piece, such as Pachelbel's "Canon in D," may also be suitable. (Suggestion: A week before the first day of class, ask a student to select some appropriate music.)

Before beginning, light a candle in the center of the group or at another appropriate focal point.

First Reader:

Let us begin with the sign of the cross: In the name of the Father, and of the Son, and of the Holy Spirit. Amen.

Loving God, we thank you for the summer which is coming to an end. As we begin a new school year, help us to return to our books, classes, and other school activities with a renewed dedication to learning. We pray in the name of Jesus, the Lord.

All Respond: Amen.

Second Reader:

A reading from the Gospel of Matthew:

[Jesus said:] "You are the salt of the earth; but if salt has lost its taste, how can its saltiness be restored? It is no longer good for anything, but is thrown out and trampled under foot.

"You are the light of the world. A city built on a hill cannot be hid.

"No one after lighting a lamp puts it under the bushel basket, but on the lampstand, and it gives light to all in the house. In the same way, let your light shine before others, so that they may see your good works and give glory to your Father in heaven" (5:13-16).

[At this point, play the recorded music selected earlier.]

Third Reader:

Now let us offer our prayers of petition for the beginning of this new school year. Our response will be, "Lord, hear our prayer."

[Students who prepared prayers of petition mention them now, then allow for any spontaneous prayers of petition to be mentioned. Each petition should conclude with, "Let us pray to the Lord."]

[After all the prayers of petition have been spoken:]

Loving God, we know that you hear our prayers even before we speak them. Hear these prayers, then, as well as all the prayers that remain in our hearts. Help us to rely on you in all things and trust in your love above everything else in the world. We pray in the name of Jesus, the Lord.

All Respond: Amen.

First Reader:

Let us return now to our regular daily activities in the peace and joy of Christ.

All Respond: Thanks be to God.

Prayer Service for Reconciliation

This prayer service is designed for use with a group of any size, in virtually any setting, including a classroom. The sacrament of reconciliation may or may not be made available depending on the particular situation.

Materials needed: candle, recorded background music (optional), a poem or story on the theme of reconciliation (see below).

Before beginning, light a candle in the center of the group or at another appropriate focal point.

First Reader:

We begin with the sign of the cross: In the name of the Father, and of the Son, and of the Holy Spirit.

Let us quiet ourselves and be at peace. As we become quiet, let us recall that our loving God dwells among us and within each one of us. This lighted candle is a sign of God's presence. Take a moment to be aware of God's loving presence in yourself and in all of us gathered here.

All Respond: God's love is in our hearts and in our midst.

Second Reader:

(Read a poem or story on the theme of reconciliation written by the reader himself or herself. This could be a short essay written as a class assignment, a first-person essay, a poem about an experience of forgiveness and reconciliation, or any other suitable student project. Alternately, read Luke 15:4-10, as follows.)

A reading from the Gospel of Luke.

[Jesus said:] "Which one of you, having a hundred sheep and losing one of them, does not leave the ninety-nine in the wilderness and go after the one that is lost until he finds it? When he has found it, he lays it on his shoulders and rejoices. And when he comes home, he calls together his friends and neighbors, saying to them, 'Rejoice with me, for I have found my sheep that was lost.' Just so, I tell you, there will be more joy in heaven over one sinner who repents than over ninety-nine righteous persons who need no repentance. "Or what woman having ten silver coins, if she loses one of them, does not light a lamp, sweep the house, and search carefully until she finds it? When she has found it, she calls together her friends and neighbors, saying, 'Rejoice with me, for I have found the coin that I had lost.' Just so, I tell you, there is joy in the presence of the angels of God over one sinner who repents."

The word of the Lord.

All Respond: Thanks be to God.

Third Reader:

We all make thoughtless or stupid choices sometimes. Now and then we choose to be selfish, to make cruel remarks about others, to forget that God's love can always be trusted. Sometimes we give the adults in our life disrespect, forgetting how much they love and care for us. Sometimes we fail to respect ourselves and those we live and work with, overlooking how deeply God loves us and them. Sometimes we fail to respect our own and others' sexuality. Sometimes we fail to respect God's creation by polluting or damaging the earth when we could care for it in appropriate ways. Because we make such choices we need to ask forgiveness and be reconciled with one another and with our loving God. Let's take a few moments to recall ways we may have distanced ourselves from God, from brothers and sisters, friends, parents, teachers, fellow students, or coworkers, or from God's good creation.

(Pause.)

Now we extinguish the candle as a sign of our separation from one another and from God through our own free choices. (Extinguish candle.)

First Reader:

(Read one of the two following options.)

Now we will have the opportunity individually to receive the sacrament of reconciliation. (Give directions for doing so.)

Or

Now let us ask God to forgive us and realize that the instant we resolve to do this God has already forgiven us. At the same time, let us resolve to be at peace with anyone we may have hurt by our words or actions.

(Appropriate recorded music may be played while individuals participate in the sacrament of reconciliation or for a few minutes following the reading of the second option.)

Second Reader:

(Re-light the candle.)

Once again we light the candle as a sign of our reconciliation with God and one another.

Let us pray. God our loving Father, we thank you for the gift of forgiveness and reconciliation which is always available to us. We thank you for the gift of peace and renewed relationships with you, with one another, and with the earth. Help us always to trust in your love and forgiveness, and help us to rededicate ourselves to serving you and others.

All Respond: Amen.

Third Reader:

Let us return now to our regular daily schedule in the peace and joy of the risen Christ.

All Respond: Thanks be to God.

Prayer Service for the Beginning of Lent (Ash Wednesday)

This prayer service, for a group of any size, is meant to complement the liturgy for Ash Wednesday which includes the blessing and distribution of ashes.

Materials needed: Candle.

Before beginning, light a candle in the center of the group or at another appropriate focal point.

First Reader:

We begin with the sign of the cross: In the name of the Father, and of the Son, and of the Holy Spirit.

At the core of the Christian life is God's call to leave behind all that comes between us and God, and all that obstructs our relationships with one another. During Lent we focus on learning to be better, more faithful friends. We also look into ourselves to see if there are ways we can become more free, less self-centered, more centered on the needs of others. We open ourselves to becoming more prayerful people.

Second Reader:

As a sign of all the ways that we separate ourselves from one another and from our loving God, we extinguish this candle. For when we choose to distance ourselves from God and one another we choose darkness rather than light. (Extinguish candle.)

Third Reader:

Let us listen now to the word of God.

A reading from the Letter to the Colossians:

As God's chosen ones, holy and beloved, clothe yourselves with compassion, kindness, humility, meekness, and patience. Bear with one another and, if anyone has a complaint against another, forgive each other; just as the Lord has forgiven you, so you also must forgive. Above all, clothe yourselves with love, which binds everything together in perfect harmony. And let the peace of Christ rule in your hearts, to which indeed you were called in the one body. And be thankful. Let the word of Christ dwell in you richly; teach and admonish one another in all wisdom; and with gratitude in your hearts sing psalms, hymns, and spiritual songs to God. And whatever you do, in word or deed, do everything in the name of the Lord Jesus, giving thanks to God the Father through him (3:12-17).

The word of the Lord.

All Respond: Thanks be to God.

First Reader:

Let us pray. God our loving Father, we thank you for the gift of your Son, Jesus, who draws us closer to you and to one another.

Please respond to the following prayers by saying, "Lord, hear our prayer."

God help us to seek the light and reject the darkness. . .

During the forty days of Lent, help us to make extra efforts to be kind, compassionate, patient and forgiving. . .

Now please mention any other prayers you would like to add, either spoken or in the silence of your heart.

Second Reader:

We now re-light the candle as a symbol of our choice to seek the light of Christ in all that we do during Lent. (Light candle.)

Third Reader:

Loving God, we thank you for the gift of Lent. Help us to observe it in ways that will help us to grow closer to you, to one another, and to our families. We pray in the name of Jesus the Lord.

All Respond: Amen.

First Reader:

Let us now return to our regular activities in the peace of Christ.

All Respond: Amen.

Prayer Service to Remember the Last Supper

This prayer service may be used in a classroom or large group setting.

Materials needed: candle and meditative recorded music, such as "The Wheat Arising" or another selection from *CommonSong: Acoustic Meditations* (cassette or compact disc, Ave Maria Press, 1-800-282-1865); also quite appropriate is the second (Adagio) movement from the Concerto for Piano in F Minor (BWV 1056), by Johann Sebastian Bach, which should be available from any public library music collection. It is also possible that some currently popular music would be appropriate; plan ahead and ask a student to check into this.

Before beginning, light a candle in the center of the group or at another appropriate focal point.

First Reader:

Today we remember that before his suffering and death on the cross, Jesus gathered with his disciples for a very special supper. In the course of this meal, Jesus gave us the eucharist—the gift of his real presence among us when we gather in his name, and the gift of the whole person of the risen Christ in the eucharistic bread and wine—"body and blood, soul and divinity."

Second Reader:

A reading from the Gospel of Matthew:

While they were eating, Jesus took a loaf of bread, and after blessing it he broke it, gave it to the disciples, and said, "Take, eat; this is my body." Then he took a cup, and after giving thanks he gave it to them, saying, "Drink from it, all of you; for this is my blood of the covenant, which is poured out for many for the forgiveness of sins" (26:26-28).

The word of the Lord.

All Respond: Thanks be to God.

(At this time, play the recorded meditative music selected in advance.)

Third Reader:

God our loving Father, we thank you for the gift of the eucharist in which your Son, Jesus, shares with us the bread of life. Help us to have a deeper appreciation for the meaning of this sacrament and a deeper sensitivity to the presence of the risen Christ among us. We pray in the name of Jesus the Lord.

All Respond: Amen.

First Reader:

Let us return now to our regular schedule and activities in the peace of Christ who lives within us and among us.

All Respond: Thanks be to God.

Prayer Service to Remember Christ's Passion

The following prayer service is appropriate for either a smaller classroom gathering or a larger group.

Materials needed: recorded meditative music. There may be some currently popular music that is appropriate, or the Agnus Dei from Mozart's "Requiem" (KV 626) may be used. The latter is available on many audio cassette or compact disc recordings available from a public library or a retail store.

First Reader:

Today we recall the suffering and death of Jesus on the cross. The purpose of this day is not to encourage a morbid preoccupation with death and suffering. Rather, we remember Jesus' death in order to remind ourselves that he embraced our human nature completely, even to the point of accepting the death that all humans must experience. Jesus not only died as we all must do, he accepted deep suffering prior to death to show us that he is with us when we suffer, too. In this way, Jesus' suffering and death brought, and continue to bring, healing and liberation. For now we know that he is with us even in suffering and death.

Second Reader:

A reading from the Gospel of Mark:

So Pilate, wishing to satisfy the crowd, released Barabbas for them; and after flogging Jesus, he handed him over to be crucified.

Then the soldiers led him into the courtyard of the palace (that is, the governor's headquarters); and they called together the whole cohort. And they clothed him in a purple cloak; and after twisting some thorns into a crown, they put it on him. And they began saluting him, "Hail, King of the Jews!"

They struck his head with a reed, spat upon him, and knelt down in homage to him. After mocking him, they stripped him of the purple cloak and put his own clothes on him. Then they led him out to crucify him. They compelled a passer-by, who was coming in from the country, to carry his cross; it was Simon of Cyrene, the father of Alexander and Rufus. Then they brought Jesus to the place called Golgotha (which means the place of a skull). And they offered him wine mixed with myrrh; but he did not take it. And they crucified him, and divided his clothes among them, casting lots to decide what each should take (15:15-24).

(At this time play the recorded meditative music selected earlier.)

Third Reader:

The response to each prayer is, "Lord, have mercy."

Let us remember the ways in which unjust suffering touches the lives of so many people in our world today, both in our own country and around the world. . .

Let us remember those who suffer from terminal illnesses, that they may feel the presence of Christ in their lives and in their relationships with others. . .

Let us remember the countless children in our world who suffer from the cruelty of hunger and war. . .

Let us remember people in our own families and community who cannot escape suffering, that they may know God's love in us and in our prayerful concern for them. . .

First Reader:

God our loving Father, we thank you for the gift of your Son, Jesus, who came to share in our human existence even to the point of accepting suffering and death. Help us to allow him to guide us in all that we do.

All Respond: Amen.

Second Reader:

Let us return now to our regular schedule and activities in the peace of the risen Christ who lives within us and among us.

All Respond: Thanks be to God.

Prayer Service for the End of the School Year

The end of the school year is a time when it's difficult to be patient, so this prayer service is purposely short and to the point, yet it gives students a chance to recognize the holiness of their feelings and experience. This service is suitable for any size group.

Materials needed: candle.

Before beginning, light a candle in the center of the group or at another appropriate focal point.

First Reader:

Today we celebrate the end of the school year and the beginning of the summer vacation. We give thanks for the past school year, and we pray to remember God's unconditional love for us, now, during the summer months, and always. The lighted candle reminds us of the presence of the risen Christ.

Second Reader:

A reading from the Book of Genesis:

So Noah went out with his sons and his wife and his sons' wives. And every animal, every creeping thing, and every bird, everything that moves on the earth, went out of the ark by families. Then Noah built an altar to the Lord, and took of every clean animal and of every clean bird, and offered burnt offerings on the altar. And when the Lord smelled the pleasing odor, the Lord said in his heart, "I will never again curse the ground because of humankind, for the inclination of the human heart is evil from youth; nor will I ever again destroy every living creature as I have done. As long as the earth endures, seedtime and harvest, cold and heat, summer and winter, day and night, shall not cease" (8:18-22).

The word of the Lord.

All Respond: Thanks be to God.

Third Reader:

The response to the prayers is, "Lord, hear our prayer."

For a happy and refreshing summer, let us pray to the Lord. . .

For a summer free from violence, let us pray to the Lord. . .

That those who are looking for summer jobs may find work, let us pray to the Lord. . .

Please add any other prayers of petition at this time. (Pause.)

God our loving Father, hear our prayers and help us to stay close to you all summer long. We pray in the name of Jesus, the Lord.

All Respond: Amen.

Reproducible Section

The pages in the following section are intended to be duplicated in conjunction with the prayer services in this book. Those who have purchased this book may feel free to copy them for use with these services without the permission of the publisher.

Prayer Service for Beginning the School Year

Prayer

All Respond: Amen.

A reading from the Gospel of Matthew

Musical Meditation

Prayers of Petition

The response to each prayer is: "Lord, hear our prayer"

Final Prayer

All Respond: Amen.

Dismissal

All Respond: Thanks be to God.

Prayer Service for Reconciliation

Prayer

All Respond: God's love is in our midst and in my heart.

Reconciliation Meditation

Recollection of our Separation from God and Others

Sign of Separation

Reconciliation

Sign of Reconciliation

Final Prayer

 All Respond: Amen.

Dismissal

All Respond: Thanks be to God.

Prayer Service for the Beginning of Lent (Ash Wednesday)

Lenten Meditation

Sign of Our Separation from God and Others

A reading from the Letter to the Colossians

All Respond: Thanks be to God.

Prayers

Sign of Our Commitment to Seek Christ's Light

Final Prayer

All Respond: Amen.

Dismissal

All Respond: Amen.

Prayer Service to Remember the Last Supper

Eucharistic Meditation

A reading from the Gospel of Matthew

All Respond: Thanks be to God.

Musical Meditation

Prayer

All Respond: Amen.

Dismissal

All Respond: Thanks be to God.

Prayer Service to Remember Christ's Passion

Meditation on Jesus' Death

A reading from the Gospel of Mark

Musical Meditation

Prayers

The response to each prayer is: "Lord, have mercy."

Prayer

All Respond: Amen.

Dismissal

All Respond: Thanks be to God.

Prayer Service for the End of the School Year

Brief Meditation on the End of the School Year

A reading from the Book of Genesis

All Respond: Thanks be to God.

Prayers

The response to the prayers is: "Lord, hear our prayer."

Final Prayer

All Respond: Amen.

Index of Prayers

(This chart included here will allow you to note the date on which particular prayers were used, if you choose.)

For Friends	23				
For Those Who Feel Lonely	23				
On Eliminating Gossip	23				
For Peace in Our School	24				
For Equality	24				
Prayers for Those in Our School Community					
For the Freshman Class	27				
For the Sophomore Class	27				
For the Junior Class	28				
For the Senior Class	28				
In Appreciation of Non-Conformists	28				
For Those Struggling with Depression	29				
For Anyone Thinking of Suicide	29				
For Teachers	29				
For Our Principal	30				
For the Office Staff	30				
For the Custodial Staff	30				
For the Yearbook Staff	31				
For the School Newspaper Staff	31				
For Coaches	31				
For Cheerleaders	32				
For Athletic Opponents	32				
For Referees	32				
Prayers for World Concerns For Peace in the World	35				

Ash Wednesday	72				
First Week of Lent	73				
Second Week of Lent	73				
Third Week of Lent	73				
Fourth Week of Lent	74				
Fifth Week of Lent	74				
Sixth Week of Lent	74				
Holy Thursday	75				
Good Friday	75				
Before Easter Break	75				
Ascension of the Lord	76				
Pentecost	76				
Prayers for Holidays Feast of the Assumption (Aug.15)	79				
First Day of Autumn	79				
Columbus Day	79				
Halloween	80				
Feast of All Saints (Nov. 1)	80				
Feast of All Souls (Nov. 2)	80				
Election Day	81				
Veterans Day	81				
Before Thanksgiving Break	81				
Feast of the Immaculate Conception (Dec. 8)	82				
First Day of Winter	82				